INSIDE YOUR BODY

ALL ABOUT BROKEN BONES

FRANCESCA POTTS, RN

Consulting Editor, Diane Craig, MA/Reading Specialist

Super Sandcastle

An Imprint of Abdo Publishing
abdopublishing.com

ABDOPUBLISHING.COM

NOV 1 5 2017

Published by Abdo Publishing, a division of ABDO, PO Box 398166, Minneapolis, Minnesota 55439. Copyright © 2018 by Abdo Consulting Group, Inc. International copyrights reserved in all countries. No part of this book may be reproduced in any form without written permission from the publisher. Super SandCastle™ is a trademark and logo of Abdo Publishing.

Printed in the United States of America,
North Mankato, Minnesota
062017
092017

THIS BOOK CONTAINS
RECYCLED MATERIALS

Production: Mighty Media, Inc.
Editor: Liz Salzmann
Cover Photographs: Shutterstock
Interior Photographs: iStockphoto, Shutterstock

Publisher's Cataloging-in-Publication Data

Names: Potts, Francesca, author.
Title: All about broken bones / by Francesca Potts, RN.
Description: Minneapolis, MN : Abdo Publishing, 2018. I Series:
    Inside your body
Identifiers: LCCN 2016962891 I ISBN 9781532111167 (lib. bdg.) I
    ISBN 9781680789010 (ebook)
Subjects: LCSH: Bones--Wounds and injuries--Juvenile literature.
    I Fractures--Juvenile literature. I Joints--Wounds and injuries--
    Juvenile literature.
Classification: DDC 617.1/5--dc23
LC record available at http://lccn.loc.gov/2016962891

Super SandCastle™ books are created by a team of professional educators, reading specialists, and content developers around five essential components—phonemic awareness, phonics, vocabulary, text comprehension, and fluency—to assist young readers as they develop reading skills and strategies and increase their general knowledge. All books are written, reviewed, and leveled for guided reading, early reading intervention, and Accelerated Reader™ programs for use in shared, guided, and independent reading and writing activities to support a balanced approach to literacy instruction.

CONTENTS

YOUR BODY

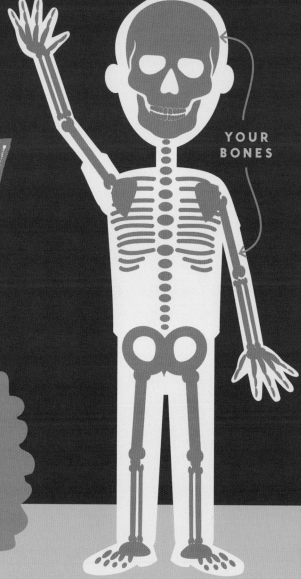

YOUR
BONES

You're amazing! So is your body.
Most of the time your body works just fine.
It lets you go to school, play with friends,
and more. But sometimes you feel sick or
part of you hurts.

Breaking a bone is one way your body can get hurt. A broken bone is very painful. But it almost always heals well. Most people break at least one bone during their lifetimes.

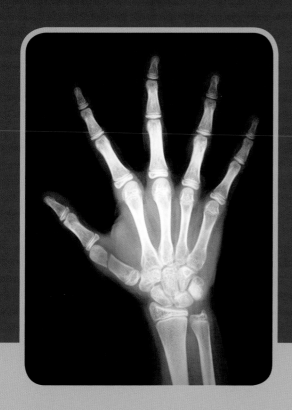

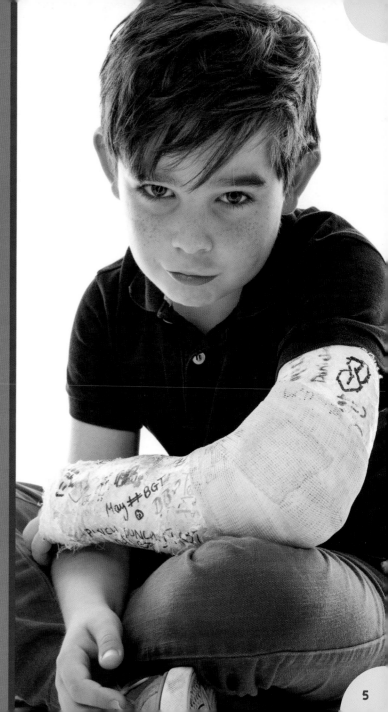

ALL ABOUT YOUR BONES

Your bones make up your skeleton. Bones are hard and stiff. **Ligaments** and **tendons** hold your skeleton and muscles together. Your skeleton is what supports your body. Without it, you wouldn't be able to walk, stand, or sit.

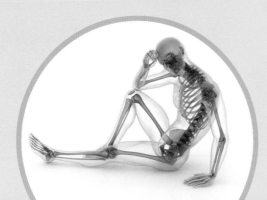

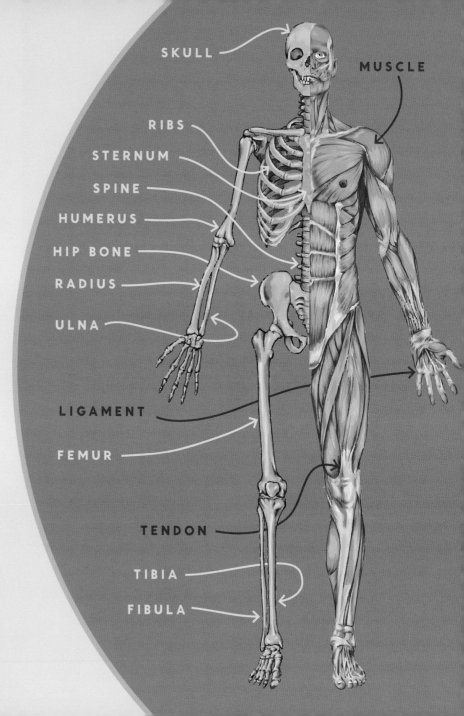

SKULL

MUSCLE

RIBS

STERNUM

SPINE

HUMERUS

HIP BONE

RADIUS

ULNA

LIGAMENT

FEMUR

TENDON

TIBIA

FIBULA

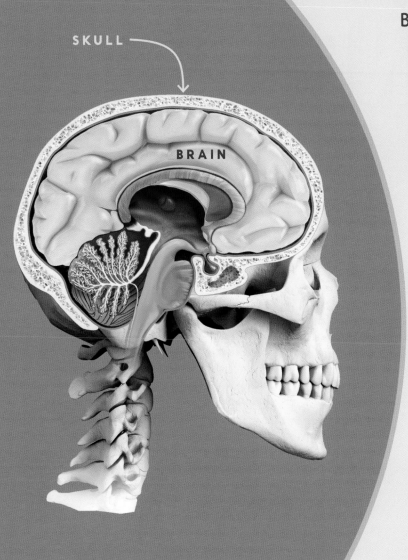

SKULL

BRAIN

Bones also protect the organs in your body. Your **skull** is made of bone. It keeps your brain from being harmed when you bump your head. Your spine and ribs are made of bones. Together, they protect your lungs and heart.

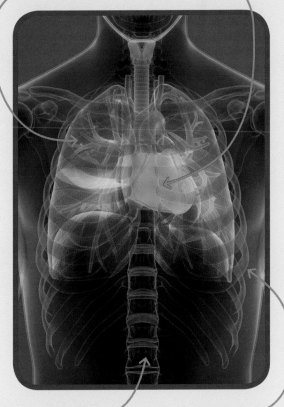

LUNGS   HEART

SPINE   RIBS

TYPES OF
BONES

THE HUMAN BODY HAS FOUR BASIC TYPES OF BONES.

Flat Bones

Flat bones are thin and broad. Your **sternum** and **skull** are flat bones.

Irregular Bones

Irregular bones aren't shaped like long, short, or flat bones. Your kneecaps are irregular bones. So are the bones of your spine.

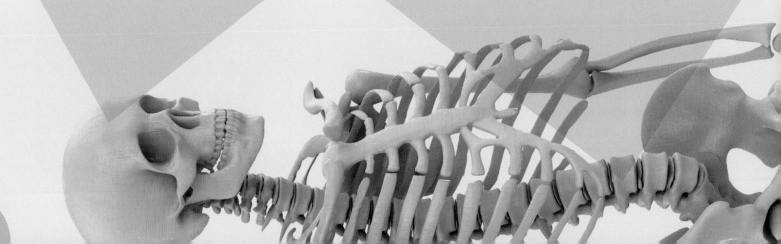

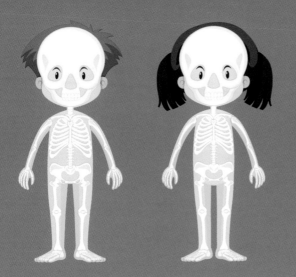

You were born with 300 bones. But some of them join together as you grow. Adults have 206 bones.

Long Bones

Long bones are long, thick, and straight. The bones in your arms and legs are long bones.

Short Bones

Short bones are shaped like long bones. But they are much smaller. The bones in your wrists and ankles are short bones.

BONES BREAK?

Bones are hard and strong. They are not easy to break. A strong force is needed to cause a broken bone. There are several common ways bones get broken.

GETTING HURT WHILE
PLAYING A SPORT

BEING IN A CAR ACCIDENT

FALLING OR JUMPING
FROM A HIGH PLACE

TWISTING AN ANKLE

SIGNS OF A
BROKEN BONE

Ask these questions if you get hurt.

- Did you hear a snap or crunch sound when you got hurt?

- Are you unable to move the hurt part of your body?

- Is the area near the bone swollen?

- Is the hurt part of your body bent the wrong way?

- Is the bone sticking out so you can see it?

Did you answer "yes" to any of these questions? If so, your bone could be broken. It will be very painful. But try to stay calm. Keep the hurt area as still as possible.

Having a broken bone is an emergency!

You need to see a doctor right away. An adult can take you to a clinic or hospital. Or call 9-1-1. Tell the person who answers what happened. He or she will send help.

FRACTURES

Doctors call broken bones *bone fractures*. There are different types of fractures. The doctor will take **X-rays** so he or she can look at your bones. The X-rays will show what type of bone fracture you have.

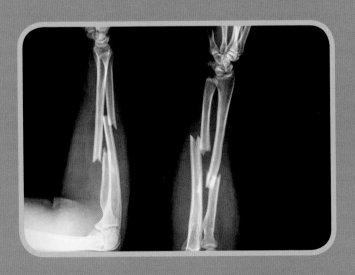

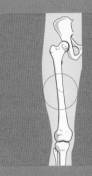

HAIRLINE FRACTURE
The bone has a very thin crack. This is also called a stress fracture.

CLOSED FRACTURE
The bone is completely broken but does not break through the skin.

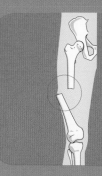

OPEN FRACTURE
The bone is broken and breaks through the skin.

COMMINUTED FRACTURE
The bone is broken into many pieces.

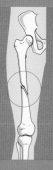

NON-DISPLACED FRACTURE
The bone is in two pieces but the ends are lined up.

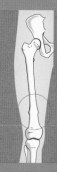

BUCKLE FRACTURE
The bone is bent but not broken.

DISPLACED FRACTURE
The bone is in two pieces and the ends are not lined up.

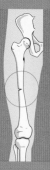

GREENSTICK FRACTURE
One side of the bone bends. The other side breaks completely.

TREATMENT

There are several **treatments** for broken bones. All of them hold the bone in its correct position. Then the bone can grow back into one piece.

CAST

A cast is often used to help a bone heal. The pieces of the bone are lined up. Then the pieces are held in place by a hard cast. The cast may also cover nearby joints. This keeps the whole area still.

SLING

A sling is a cloth that supports a hurt limb. It helps keep the limb still. A sling can be used along with a cast or splint.

SPLINT

A splint can be used for a broken limb or digit. A splint is a stiff board. It is tied to the broken limb. This holds the limb straight. Sometimes, a broken digit is taped to the one next to it instead. The healthy digit acts like a splint.

SURGERY

A severe break can require **surgery**. The surgeon uses pins to hold the pieces of the bone in position. Then a cast is applied.

MEDICATION

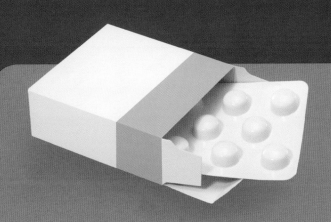

Pain Medicine

There are medicines that can reduce pain and swelling.

Antibiotics

Some broken bones get **infected**. An infection may spread to other parts of the body. An **antibiotic** can prevent or cure an infection.

THERAPY

Physical therapy is exercise that helps with healing. While a bone heals, you can't use that part of your body. So, the muscles in that area can become weak. Physical therapy helps strengthen them again.

STRAINS AND SPRAINS

You can also hurt body parts that are connected to bones. These include muscles, **ligaments**, and **tendons**. A strain is when a muscle gets stretched too far. A sprain is when a ligament or tendon is partly torn.

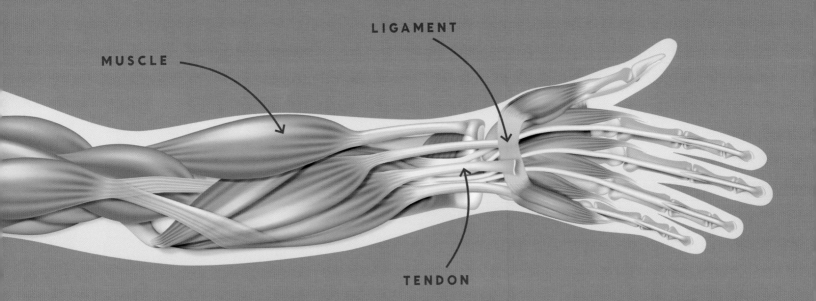

LIGAMENT

MUSCLE

TENDON

Strains and sprains are very painful. But they are often less serious than broken bones. Strains and sprains can usually be treated at home. The best **treatment** for them is R.I.C.E. This stands for Rest, Ice, Compression, Elevation.

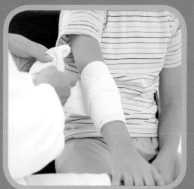 

Rest

Keep the hurt area as still as possible. Moving can make it worse. Also, when you rest, you use less energy. So, your body will have more energy for healing.

Ice

Ice helps with pain and swelling. Wrap ice in a cloth. Press it to the hurt area for 20 minutes, several times a day.

Compression

Wrap the hurt area tightly. This will support it and keep it still.

Elevation

Elevating a hurt part of the body can reduce swelling. It reduces the amount of blood flowing to the area. Elevation is used for hurt arms, legs, and feet.

PREVENTION

I t is important to remember that accidents happen! They are unexpected and hard to stop. But there are ways to help prevent your bones from breaking.

Exercise

Being active helps your bones and muscles stay strong.

Calcium

Calcium is a natural element. It makes your bones strong. So, eat foods that have a lot of calcium. This includes dairy foods and green vegetables.

Safety Gear

Protect your bones with safety gear such as helmets and knee pads. And always wear a seatbelt when you are in a car. If necessary, use a booster seat too.

ANTIBIOTIC – a substance used to kill germs that cause disease.

INFECTION – an unhealthy condition caused by bacteria or other germs. If something has an infection, it is infected.

IRREGULAR – not evenly or uniformly shaped, arranged, or spaced.

LIGAMENT – a band of tough fibers that joins two bones together.

SKULL – the bones that protect the brain and form the face.

STERNUM – a flat bone in the chest that the rib bones are connected to.

SURGERY – the treating of sickness or injury by cutting into and repairing body parts. A doctor who performs surgery is a surgeon.

TENDON – a band of tough fibers that joins a muscle to another body part, such as a bone.

TREATMENT – medical or surgical care for a sickness or an injury.

X-RAY – a photograph of the inside of the body or another object.

GLOSSARY